THE REALITY DISTORTION FIELD

CHANGE THE WORLD BY CONVINCING OTHERS TO SHARE YOUR DREAM

BY
SHAWN CARSON

CHANGING MIND PUBLISHING
NEW YORK, NY

CONTENTS

Foreword- 4

Introduction- 6

Chapter 1: The Reality Distortion Field- 8

Chapter 2: The Art of Genius- 11

Chapter 3: Locus of Control- 18

Chapter 4: Nonconsensus Reality- 33

Chapter 5: The Art of Non-negotiation- 38

Chapter 6: Dealing with Failure- 42

Chapter 7: The Art of Out Framing- 49

Chapter 8: Preframes and Inoculation- 53

Chapter 9: Leveraging Values- 58

Chapter 10: Layering Realities- 64

Chapter 11: Stealing Ground- 66

Chapter 12: Physiology of RDF- 70

Chapter 13: The Secret of Congruence- 74

Chapter 14: Paying Attention to Your Audience- 78

Chapter 15: Keeping Your Outcome in Mind- 81

Chapter 16: Putting It Together- 85

Conclusion- 93

FOREWORD

BY JESS MARION

Steve Jobs has touched the lives of countless millions of people around the world, myself included. Since I was small, Apple has been a part of my life. The first computer I learned to type on in first grade was a Mac. Being a child of the 90s, I grew up watching Pixar films thanks to Steve Jobs. Even today I feel like my iPhone is an extension of myself and my MacBook a trusted friend who helps me get work done and have fun, rather than them being just tools.

This love affair with Apple that myself and so many other people are in took me down a very interesting road in 2014. It was at that time that Shawn and I were deeply enmeshed in the world of Deep Trance Identification. As a part of our research both he and I set out on separate modeling projects with Steve jobs. I was interested in the modals by which Jobs lived his life while Shawn was deeply fascinated by the Reality Distortion Field. One of the outcomes of Shawn's modeling project is the book you're currently reading.

I was honored and very excited to be asked to write the foreword for this book not only because of my own interest in Steve Jobs as a DTI model but also because of how Jobs was able to completely change the face of the world. His genius and unrelenting personality drove his company to create products that are beyond utilitarian; they inspire love.

Jobs was able to motivate his teams to create the impossible. He also showed the world a new way of relating to technology and each other.

As you begin this book you are embarking on an adventure that can transform your life, your world, and the reality of everyone touched by your dream. You will develop the inner landscape and skills to create your own Reality Distortion Field just as Steve Jobs did. Shawn has taken the RDF, something others have only been on the effect side of, and has elegantly distilled it down to method that you can begin using to live your dreams. Dream big because you are dreaming for all of us!

Be warned that as you go forward in this book you will not be able to look at the world or your goals the same way ever again. The experience is like moving from a rotary phone to an iPhone in one single step. Only proceed forward when you are absolutely ready to take control of your reality in a way that allows you to dream big, and live that dream.

It is my deepest wish that you enjoy the Reality Distortion Field, and get as much out of the exercises in the book, as I have. I don't know exactly in what ways reality can bend for you to live your dreams, but I do know that it is a lot of fun to find out. As Neo was told in the Matrix, it's not the spoon that bends, it's yourself.

INTRODUCTION

"The people who are crazy enough to think they can change the world are the ones who do."

"Here's to the crazy ones. The misfits. The rebels. The troublemakers. The round pegs in the square holes. The ones who see things differently. They're not fond of rules. And they have no respect for the status quo. You can quote them, disagree with them, glorify or vilify them. About the only thing you can't do is ignore them. Because they change things. They push the human race forward. And while some may see them as the crazy ones, we see genius. Because the people who are crazy enough to think they can change the world are the ones who do."

—Rob Siltanen, copywriter, "The Crazy Ones" ad for Apple computer

Perhaps you are a Mac user; you have a PC in the office but prefer a Mac at home. Or maybe you have an iPhone, or perhaps an iPad. Maybe you use iTunes, or you used to have an iPod. If you live in the United States, or indeed in the Western world, it's likely that you own or have owned a product manufactured by Apple, the company founded by Steve Jobs and his partner Steve Wozniak. Apple became a global titan in the technology industry through the power of Steve Jobs's vision and his ability to persuade those around him that his vision was reality even when that reality was "impossible"' by anyone else's standards.

Even if you have never owned a Mac, iPod, iPhone, or iPad, you may have seen the movie Toy Story or Monsters Inc. or the recent Inside Out. These movies were all created by Pixar, the company that

Steve Jobs rescued from bankruptcy and turned into a powerhouse of the movie industry. Pixar was later bought by Disney, making Steve Jobs one of the largest Disney shareholders at that time.

This ability that Steve Jobs possessed, to persuade others that the impossible is not only possible but inevitable, was known as Jobs's Reality Distortion Field (RDF).

You may know someone who has this ability to persuade, to a greater or lesser degree. In my experience, the Reality Distortion Field comes in two main flavors. The first is the snake-oil salesman. He understands the principles of the Reality Distortion Field and chooses to use his talents for his own purposes. These purposes may be small and petty, like selling Florida swampland. Or his purpose may be grandiose yet deranged, perhaps a cult leader, or even a dictator.

If you want to be one of these people, then this is not the book for you. But by reading this book, playing through the exercises, and applying everything you will learn to the observation of others, you will find yourself in a position to see through the snake-oil salesman by identifying the RDF as it is spun.

Fortunately, there is another kind of RDF. This is the kind used by Steve Jobs to transform the world of technology. And it has been used by other transformative figures from Socrates to Cicero, Gandhi to Martin Luther King, Jr., anyone who dreamed a dream into reality, not just for themselves, but for the world.

I hope you have a dream of a better world. A world where everyone is wiser, bolder, more creative, more loving, more spiritual. This book is intended for those who choose to turn their dreams into reality.

CHAPTER 1
THE   REALITY   DISTORTION FIELD

"A charismatic rhetorical style, an indomitable will, and an eagerness to bend any fact to fit the purpose at hand."

"The Reality Distortion Field was a confounding melange of a charismatic rhetorical style, an indomitable will, and an eagerness to bend any fact to fit the purpose at hand. If one line of argument failed to persuade, he would deftly switch to another. ... Amazingly, the Reality Distortion Field seemed to be effective even if you were acutely aware of it, although the effects would fade after Steve departed."

—Andy Hertzfeld, Apple employee

If you had worked for Apple in the 1970s or early 1980s, and had been fortunate enough to work with Steve Jobs, for example, on the Apple or Mac computer projects, then you would have had the opportunity to experience Steve Jobs's Reality Distortion Field firsthand. Those who did have this experience reported the effect as being so strong that Jobs could make them believe the impossible was possible, and that even insurmountable obstacles could be overcome.

Being computer geeks, Jobs's colleagues naturally named the effect in honor of an episode of the popular science fiction program *Star Trek*. In this episode, called "The Menagerie," the crew of the starship

Enterprise comes face to face with an alien race that was able to control its perception of reality.

> "It was a perfect illusion. They had us seeing just want we wanted to see ... everything entirely logical ... everything. Now, let's be sure we understand the danger of this: [they] can read our minds; they can create illusions out of a person's own thoughts, memories and experiences, even out of a person's own desires, illusions just as real and solid as this table top and just as impossible to ignore."
>
> —Dr. Boyce, Star Trek "The Menagerie"

In this book, we explore the elements that made Steve Jobs's Reality Distortion Field possible. I explain the five personal characteristics of Steve Jobs that made him such a great communicator. I'll show you the five elements to consider when crafting your own RDF. And I'll tell you the five behaviors you will need to deliver your RDF to your chosen audience. Five personal characteristics, five elements, and five behaviors—15 keys in all. Once you have mastered each of these areas, you too can harness the power of the Reality Distortion Field to achieve your own goals and dreams.

Without the ability to persuade others, you will be no more than an also-ran in the game of life. I'm not saying it is going to be easy to become a master communicator and influencer. However, if you master only one or two of the 15 keys, I guarantee you can become an even more powerful and more persuasive communicator than you are now. The ability to persuade others is a key skill in our interconnected world, one that takes hard work and, yes, a little bit of luck. And with these 15 keys, you can unlock the gateway and reach the pinnacle of success.

So, sit back, fasten your seatbelt, and prepare yourself for a trip to the Reality Distortion Field!

CHAPTER 2
THE ART OF GENIUS

"Some may see them as crazy."

> "Here's to the crazy ones. ... Maybe they have to
> be crazy. How else can you stare at an empty
> canvas and see a work of art? Or sit in silence
> and hear a song that's never been written? Or
> gaze at a red planet and see a laboratory on
> wheels?
> —Rob Siltanen, "The Crazy Ones" (full
> version)

How often do you hear the words, "That can't be done"? Or, "That's impossible"? These are the sorts of rules the crazy ones disregard.

Steve Jobs had an engineer on his team who came up with a design for the Macintosh based on what was possible. Steve Jobs told him to think of anything and everything he would like to see in the Mac, especially the impossible, and then build that instead. The engineer wrote a sarcastic email to Jobs describing the functions of this impossible computer, ending with the statement that it couldn't be built. Steve Jobs fired him practically on the spot. The Macintosh computer included most of the "impossible" features the engineer described in the memo.

As President John Kennedy understood when he committed the United States to sending the first man to the moon, setting impossible goals can motivate people to achieve the (almost) impossible:

"We choose to go to the moon. We choose to go to the moon in this decade and do the other things, not because they are easy, but because they are hard, because that goal will serve to organize and measure the best of our energies and skills, because that challenge is one that we are willing to accept, one we are unwilling to postpone, and one which we intend to win"
—John F. Kennedy

Steve Jobs might have set impossible goals for his teams—I mean *really* impossible goals. Indeed, Jobs and his product development teams were notorious for missing their self-imposed deadlines and for producing products that fell well short of Jobs's hyperbole. Nevertheless, the products produced, such as the Mac, were exceptional and improved over time. More often than not, these products have proven to be unique and amazing tools that had not even been contemplated before Steve Jobs.

Steve Jobs changed the world by changing the relationship people have with technology. He believed (rightly) that if he provided the right tool, people would find amazing and creative ways of using it. He also understood, on a deeper level, that to do this, people had to be seduced by the beauty of the tools he provided; the tools had to become part of the person. (This morning I was waiting to cross the street in New York City and saw a young lady almost get run down because she was engrossed in texting. Her iPhone had become fused with her hand, eye, and brain, more a part of her existence than the traffic hurtling toward her!)

So how did Steve Jobs seduce the world? Steve Jobs seduced all of us by allowing him self to become seduced first, seduced by the technology he dreamed into existence. When you watch his presentations for new Apple products, you will clearly see this (see YouTube).

But Steve Jobs and Apple are not the only examples of these seismic changes.

Becoming the Change: Generating Genius

If I asked you to transform the world simply by waking people up, you would probably think it was impossible. Yet the Buddha changed the world not just by believing that we sleep through our lives but also by believing he could wake himself up, and by waking himself, teaching his followers to do the same.

If I ask you to transform the world by choosing one simple rule to live your life by, you would think it was impossible. Yet Jesus changed the world by believing that the Golden Rule (Do unto others as you would have them do unto you) is an absolute truth and acting according to the absolute truth of this rule.

If I asked you to transform the world by doing nothing, you would probably think it was impossible. Yet Gandhi changed the world by simply refusing to do what he was told by those in power. Gandhi became the change he wanted to see in the world, and he changed the world as a result.

You see, you don't need to believe in the impossible to change the world. You simply need to act consistently and congruently *as if* the world you want to see already exists. You have to believe in a Big Dream, and by believing, act as if it's already true in order to inspire others.

Exercise 1: Finding Your Dream

Perhaps you're lucky enough to have a Big Dream. Don't worry if you don't because I'm going to show you how to find it. In fact, using this method you can generate the biggest dream that lives inside you, the thing you were born to do.

All you need to begin is a goal, an outcome, something you want to achieve even if it's apparently something small. Take a few moments and find a goal; write it down here or in your notebook.

My goal:

Now I'm going to ask you an important question, and it's not about you, and it's not about your goal: If someone else could achieve your goal, someone who would not think it was possible for him but he got it anyway, what would that do for him that's bigger than just the goal? How would his life be transformed? Write down the answer here or in your notebook.

If another person could achieve my goal, someone who would not think it possible for him, it would give him:

Now I want you to see that person with this gift. But multiply it by 2 or 10 or 100. It may help to ask yourself: Where else might this lead her? What else would be possible for her? And where would that lead her? Write down the answer here or in your notebook.

The big benefit to her could be:

Now imagine that everyone, literally everyone, in the world had this big benefit. How would the world be different? Write down your answer here or in your notebook.

When everyone has this big benefit, the big benefit to the world will be:

Now do the same thing with another of your goals.

Goal:

Benefit to another person:

Big benefit:

Big benefit to the world:

Now do the same thing with another of your goals.

Goal:

Benefit to another person:

Big benefit:

Big benefit to the world:

When you do this a few times, you will begin to see the big picture, the pattern that repeats itself through all your goals when applied to everyone. This is the Big Dream you were born to dream into existence!

CHAPTER 3
LOCUS OF CONTROL

"The people who are crazy enough to believe they can change the world are the ones who do."

—Rob Siltanen, copywriter, "The Crazy Ones" ad for Apple computer

In the second part of the book, I will show you how you can construct a specific Reality Distortion Field to persuade other people to follow your dream and to cooperate in making it a reality.

But before we do that, I have to show you how to step into the role of visionary in the style of Steve Jobs. After all, if you don't have the personal characteristics of a visionary, to build a vision of the future that is compelling to everyone around you, then your skills of persuasion will be at best limited. To paraphrase, you may persuade some of the people all of the time, and you may even persuade all of the people some of the time, but you won't persuade the people you need to persuade long enough to reach your dream.

So in this section, I will talk about the personal characteristics, the five character traits, that Steve Jobs possessed that a visionary needs to generate a Reality Distortion Field in the style of Steve Jobs. And more important, I will show you how to develop these characteristics yourself. The first characteristic is your locus of control.

Locus of Control

Steve Jobs famously attended an early Apple holiday party dressed as Jesus—just one example of what many see as the hubris of Steve Jobs. After all, who was this guy who believed he could change the world? And how dare he be right about that! The model used by psychologists to describe this mindset is called *locus of control*.

At its most basic, locus of control describes whether you believe you can control the world around you. If you believe in your ability to control events, then you have a high locus of control. On the other hand, if you believe yourself at the mercy of events around you, then you have a low locus of control. Obviously, Steve Jobs's locus of control was off the charts.

In Neuro-Linguistic Programming (NLP), we talk about goals (called *outcomes* in NLP) being well formed. To be well formed, your goal has to be within your control. After all, if your goal is not within your control, you will never achieve it except through luck. For example: If your goal is to win the lottery, then you will need to be lucky no matter how much time or money you spend buying lottery tickets.

On the surface, this makes a lot of sense. But the question is, what *exactly* is under your control and what is not? It turns out that this is a very hard question to answer. What is under your control mostly depends not upon some objective reality, but rather on your own beliefs and perceptions about yourself, the world around you, and your place in the world.

If you have a low locus of control, then any goal you set for yourself will be outside of your control; you will achieve this goal only through luck. In contrast, when you have a high locus of control, you can have bigger goals that are still within your control.

Let's take an example.

Suppose your friend Tim wants to get a job with an investment bank on Wall Street, but he has a low locus of control. He might say to himself, "The economy is bad right now; investment banks are not hiring, and even if they were, there are so many people out of work who have more experience than I have I'll never get the job."

With this attitude, he would not be enthusiastic about sending out job applications. Even if he could bring himself to send out his résumé, and was lucky enough to get an interview, his body language and other unconscious communication would send a negative message to the potential employer. And when he didn't get a job offer, it would simply serve to confirm what he already knew: getting his dream job was out of his control.

Now, let's suppose you have a high locus of control and are seeking your dream job. You believe this goal is totally within your control, and you say to yourself, "I want this job. I'm going to get this job. And I'm going to do anything and everything I need to do to get this job!" You won't simply search for jobs that have been posted online because everyone else is also applying for these. Instead, you will speak to people you know, and speak to total strangers, to build connections and hence find opportunities that no one else was aware of. You will approach potential employers to have meetings to explore mutually beneficial opportunities. And when those meetings don't pan out, you will take the time to get feedback on what you could have done differently, or what other skills you need to develop to do better next time. And you will take this feedback onboard. You will hone your approach and develop new skills for the next time. In this way, you will inevitably succeed because you will adapt and improve until you do.

I have a good friend, Dirk, who works as a salesman (when he's not pursuing his passion of writing plays). Upon joining the three-person sales team for a branch of the company he works for, Dirk increased the sales for that branch by a factor of 10. Rather than passively waiting for potential customers to visit the branch, Dirk takes the attitude that sales are within his control at all times, and he builds the potential for new business everywhere he goes, even when he is not working, by building the right kind of relationships.

Exercise 2: Developing Belief in Your Ability to Control the World

To develop your locus of control, choose a particular context where you would like to be more successful; it could be in business, in your career, in your personal life. It really doesn't matter what you choose because we are using this only an exercise at this point.

Once you've chosen a context, choose a goal you would like to achieve in this context. Think about that goal, and picture it in your mind. What will you be seeing and hearing and feeling when you have achieved this goal?

Now consider whether this goal is within your control. If it is, then ask yourself, "What is stopping me from achieving it now?" If you still believe the goal is within your control, then choose a bigger goal. For the purposes of this exercise, it's best to choose a goal that you feel is totally and insanely *outside* of your control at this time. We are simply using this to develop your locus of control muscles.

Once you have this impossible goal in mind, and you can see and hear and feel what it will be like to have achieved it, begin breaking it down into smaller steps. Choose perhaps three to five smaller steps that will lead to your goal.

1. What do I have to do first?

2. What do I have to do next?

3. And so on until you reach your goal.

Now consider what you will do if your first step doesn't succeed in the way you want:

- How will I have to respond in the moment?

- How will I discover what went wrong?

- How will I know what I will have to do differently to make this step work?

You won't be able to consider every eventuality, but you do want to have the ability to respond flexibly to whatever may happen. Do the same thing with the second step and with the rest of the steps.

Now consider the first step you have to take to reach your goal, including the actions you'll take, if things don't go your way. Is this first step, and alternative actions, within your control? Note which ones feel as though they are and which ones feel as though they are not.

Now take any of the steps or actions that you still feel are *not* within your control. Break each of these down into three to five smaller steps in the same way you did before. Consider how you will respond if they don't go your way.

Consider each of the smaller steps. Are they all under your control? Or are some of them still not under your control? Take the ones that are not under your control and break them down into three to five even smaller steps.

If you're not used to thinking in this way, you may have to break each step and each action down to something that might take you only a few seconds. Perhaps in one of your steps you need to call someone and ask for a meeting. Perhaps you feel this is not under your control. What about if you make your first action picking up your phone? Can you do this? Is it under your control? Of course, the answer is yes. Now you have to dial the telephone number. Is that under your control? If not, break it down further. Can you dial the area code? Whatever it is, break it down into steps that are small enough that you feel they are completely under your control.

And know how you will respond if things don't go the way you hope. For example: You want to call someone and ask for a meeting. You've broken it down into smaller steps with alternative responses:

1. Pick up the phone.
2. Dial the number.

3. Ask for Mr. Smith.

4. Introduce yourself.

5. Ask for the meeting.

6. Explain why it will be beneficial for Mr. Smith.

7. And so on.

What will you do if the call rings through to voicemail? What will you say if you get through to the company's receptionist, not Mr. Smith? What about if you get through to his personal assistant? What will you say if he refuses to meet with you?

Make sure each of the steps and your alternative responses are within your control.

I'm not talking about their being under your control on an intellectual level, but on an emotional level as well. And you know what you're going to do if things don't go exactly according to plan. Again, you can't cover every eventuality, but by thinking in this way, you can begin to build up the strength of your locus of control as well as your behavioral flexibility to deal with whatever comes up.

When you have the steps mapped out, begin to link them up again into larger actions. Run the scenario like a movie in your mind:

- First step
- Second step
    - First eventuality
    - Second eventuality
- Third step

And because each smaller step eventuality is under your control, any chain of steps is also under your control. All you have to do is to put one foot in front of the other enough times and you'll reach your goal.

Exercise 3: Locus of Control and Your Big Dream

Now it's time to apply this technique to your Big Dream. No matter how big your Big Dream is, you can always break it down into a series of goals. In fact, the way we found your Big Dream was by using a series of smaller goals.

As you complete this exercise with each of the goals that lead to your Big Dream, break each goal down into steps and eventualities that are all emotionally and intellectually within your control. Recombine the steps into goals and the goals into your Big Dream. You will know without question that your Big Dream is also within your control!

Now write the Big Dream, goals, steps, and eventualities here or in your notebook.

Big Dream:

Goal 1:

Steps:

Eventualities:

Now do the same thing with another of your goals.

Goal 2:

Steps:

Eventualities:

Remember, this does not mean that everything is going to go according to plan. After all, Steve Jobs rarely delivered a product on time or one that matched his initial vision. But that's not the point. The point is to believe in your own ability to control the future sufficiently that other people will believe it too! Because, when they do, miracles will happen.

The Role of Faith in Locus of Control

> "You can't connect the dots looking forward; you can only connect them looking backward. So you have to *trust* that the dots will somehow connect in your future. You have to trust in something—your gut, destiny, life, karma, whatever. This approach has never let me down, and it has made all the difference in my life."
>
> —Steve Jobs

There is a second aspect, a second axis, to locus of control. This might be called faith. *Faith* is trusting that the universe will provide those things that you need to succeed.

You see, Steve Jobs believed in his own ability. He believed he could create an insanely great product, an insanely great computer, iPod, iPhone, iPad. Whatever it might be it would be awesome. But there were some things he couldn't be sure about. For example: He couldn't be sure that there would be a market for the product. After all, he was creating products that had never been made before.

So he had faith.

"Technology is nothing. What's important is that you have a faith in people, that they're basically good and smart, and if you give them tools, they'll do wonderful things with them."

—Steve Jobs

He had to have faith that people would find insanely great ways to use the insanely great products he created.

So locus of control is actually a combination of belief in yourself to create your future and faith in the universe to provide what is required to propagate that future out into the universe. These two ingredients combine to create massive locus of control, the first element of being a visionary.

Generating Faith

By building the habit of breaking your goals down into a series of next smallest steps, the next easily achievable action, you will know that they are under your control. But what about faith, the faith that the universe is going to do its part to provide the elements necessary for your success? Surely, that's not a reasonable thing to believe. After all, how can you know? Doesn't it all comes down to luck?

It turns out that there is a rational, and indeed scientific, basis for the power of faith. This is particularly true when we talk about faith that you will be lucky; those who believe themselves to be lucky are lucky.

Now, this doesn't mean that you can believe yourself to be lucky and go out and buy a lottery ticket guaranteed to win. However when you believe you are lucky, and that the universe will provide opportunities to you, it does. There is a very good scientific reason for this.

You see, believing that you're lucky opens you up to the possibility that something good will happen. But if you believe you are unlucky, you literally close yourself off from these opportunities. And because the universe actually offers you many opportunities every day, believing yourself to be lucky and opening yourself up to these possibilities guarantees that you will be lucky.

In one research study, participants were asked whether they considered themselves to be lucky. They were then asked to look through a newspaper searching for a certain word. If they found the word, they would receive some money. On a double-page spread in the middle of the newspaper was a large ad telling them that if they took the page to the experimenter at the front of the room, they would actually receive 10 times as much. The people who noticed the ad and got the additional reward were those who considered themselves to be lucky.

So to be lucky, all you have to do is to *believe* that you are. If you already believe that you're lucky, all well and good. But what do you do if you don't believe that you're lucky—yet? To build this belief that you're a lucky person, we are going to use a technique from NLP called *belief change*. This technique uses sensory markers called *submodalities* that your brain uses naturally to encode information about any situation.

By the way, people who go to Vegas to gamble away their savings are already very good at unconsciously running this pattern on themselves!

Exercise 4: NLP Belief Change

First, think of a specific context or situation where you don't believe you will be lucky. Pick a specific time on a specific day when things will go well if you're lucky but not so well if you're not, and either you're not sure you will be lucky or, even worse, you just know you won't be.

Picture that situation in your mind. As you do so, notice the following details (the submodalities) about the picture, and write them down. It may help if you have a partner to ask you the questions and write down the answers leaving you free to focus on your internal images.

- Where is the picture as you see it in your mind's eye? Is it more to the left or to the right? Is it farther up or farther down? Is it closer to you or farther away?

- How big is the picture?

- Is the picture of movie or a still?

- Is the picture framed or unframed?

- Is the picture three-dimensional, like real life, or is it two-dimensional, like a photograph?

- Is the picture bright or dim?

- Do you see yourself in the picture, or is it as if you're looking out of your own eyes?

- Is there sound associated with the picture, or is it silent?

Once you have checked out these details, put this picture to one side for now.

This time think of a situation where you know you actually were lucky, very lucky. Perhaps you won something or somebody gave you an unexpected bonus or you literally tripped over an opportunity.

Make a picture of this situation in your mind. As you look at this picture, check out the same qualities of the picture as before, and write them down side by side with the original list. Again, it may help if you have a partner to ask you the questions and write down your answers leaving you free to focus on your internal pictures.

- Where is the picture as you see it in your mind's eye? Is it more to the left or to the right? Is it farther up or farther down? Is it closer to you or farther away?
- How big is the picture?
- Is the picture a movie or a still?
- Is the picture framed or unframed?
- Is the picture three-dimensional, like real life, or is it two-dimensional, like a photograph?
- Is the picture bright or dim?
- Do you see yourself in the picture, or is it as if you're looking out of your own eyes?
- Is there sound associated with the picture, or is it silent?

Now take a look at the two lists and the qualities, first for the situation in which you believe you're going to be unlucky compared to the situation in which you know you were lucky. Notice which of the qualities is different; perhaps the picture where you know you're lucky is closer and bigger than the one where you do not believe yourself to be lucky—or vice versa. Finding the qualities that differ between different contexts is called a *contrastive analysis*.

Now I want you to go back to the first picture, the situation where you believed you would be unlucky. We are going to make two changes in this picture. Firstly, we're going to change the picture so that it shows you getting what you want, that is, luck.

But this isn't going to be enough to make you believe that you will be lucky. To do that, we have to change the *qualities* of the picture so that they match those of the picture in which you know you were lucky.

Let's assume that your lucky picture is closer and bigger than your unlucky picture, but the other qualities are the same. Take the unlucky picture and shoot it off into the distance in your imagination so that it goes far away and becomes small and dark. Then bring the picture back, as if it were attached to a piece of elastic. But when it comes back, it's going to show you being lucky, and it's going to end up in the position where you keep your lucky picture, and it's going to be exactly the same size as the lucky picture.

Now blank your internal movie screen, and do this all over again. See the unlucky situation, and send a picture off into the distance so that it becomes far away, small, and dark. Now have the picture come back, but this time it shows you being lucky and it comes back closer and bigger, like the lucky picture.

Now blank your internal movie screen, and do it again. Do this enough times so that you begin to believe that you will be lucky in that situation. This may take between five to ten repetitions, depending upon how quickly your unconscious mind generalizes this change.

Chapter 4
Nonconsensus Reality

"Sometimes I've believed six impossible things before breakfast."

> "Alice: 'There's no use in trying since one can't believe impossible things.'
> Queen: 'I dare say you haven't had much practice. When I was younger, I always did it for half an hour each day. Why, sometimes I've believed as many as six impossible things before breakfast.'"
>
> —The Red Queen from *Alice's Adventures in Wonderland*

> "Reality is a construction"
> —Presupposition of HNLP

Consensus Reality

It's fair to say that most people believe in an objective reality, a reality we all share. We feel this reality very concretely whenever we stub a toe on the way to the bathroom in the morning. Ouch!

However, my experience of that objective reality may be very different from yours. I can experience reality only through *my* senses, the things I see, hear, feel, taste, and smell. You may experience things differently.

It's also true to say that I have a good deal of control over how I experience objective reality by *choice*, by choosing to use my senses to focus on one thing versus another, how I choose to focus on it, and how I choose to interpret it.

> "The truth is out there. It will find you if you let it."
>
> —Trinity, *The Matrix*

There is so much information out there in objective reality, so many possibilities that you can rest assured your truth is out there. There are literally millions of sensory inputs available to us at any moment in time, yet we pay attention to only a handful.

Therefore, if you want something to be true, you can be open to those experiences that would make it true. And you can measure how true it is based on those experiences, interpreting those experiences in a way that supports your truth.

By this stage, you're probably asking, "Aren't I just deluding myself if I do this? Isn't it better to consider all the data to work out whether I'm right or wrong?" The answer to the question is yes, you are deluding yourself. And no, for the purposes of building your RDF, it's not better to consider all the data, just the data that support you.

Nonconsensus Reality

To construct and deliver a Reality Distortion Field, you need to convince one person above all others—and that's yourself. If *you* are not convinced of the absolute reality of your position, you can rest assured that no one else will be either! Research shows that over 90 percent of the believability of a message is delivered through body language and tone of voice, not through the words that we consciously select.

If you don't believe in your own Reality Distortion Field, then your disbelief will be seen in your body language and heard in your tone of voice. Even if you made a monumental conscious effort to hide your own disbelief, the effort itself would reveal itself through physical stress.

To master the Reality Distortion Field, you have to master your own belief. To master your own belief, you have to have a complete disregard for consensus reality, for what everybody else believes to be real. And you have to focus your attention on everything that supports your personal reality. This is known as *nonconsensus reality*.

This is not as crazy, nor as difficult, as it may sound. When Steve Jobs was developing the latest Apple product, most of the people who worked for him might have thought it was impossible to do what Steve Jobs wanted. That was the consensus reality, and that was indeed the case then.

But Steve Jobs was focused on something different, something known as *Moore's law*. Moore's law states that computing power doubles approximately every 18 months. When Steve Jobs focused his attention on Moore's law, he interpreted it as meaning that what was *impossible* now would be not only *possible* but inevitable in the near future. He designed his products according to where computing power was expected to be when the products came to market.

Similarly, by focusing your attention on those sensory experiences you have that support your personal nonconsensus reality, your Big Dream, and by ignoring any elements of consensus reality that contradict it, you can build your own belief. Your belief in your personal reality will be one of the key ingredients of your Reality Distortion Field.

(A word of warning here: Laws of physics, such as the law of gravity, are part of a different type of reality or knowledge. These physical laws are generally not subject to alteration. If you want to fly, use an airplane!)

Examples of Different Realities

Let's consider a simple example of two people, Jack and Jill, with different eating habits, but the same sensory reality and thought reality. They both experience: *Delicious smell; hmmm sweetness; looks nice; energy boost; it's only one; I've been good.*

Whenever Jack and Jill pass the donut shop, Jack goes in and buys a donut or two. Jill exerts willpower and passes by. Jack suffers later when he experiences the sugar crash, or when he looks in the mirror and notices his spare tire. But Jill suffers there and then by depriving herself in the moment.

But suppose they are joined one day by Janet. Janet has a different sensory reality and thought reality. She passes the donut shop and doesn't even notice it. When Jack brings it to her attention she experiences: *Ugh, smells artificial; yuck too sweet; makes me feel shaky; I'm glad this is so easy for me; looking forward to my yoga.*

Janet is able to bypass the temptation; it isn't even a temptation for her. Her reality blocks the possibility of having a donut because of what she focuses on and how she measures what she sees.

Exercise 5: Creating Your Nonconsensus Reality

Take a moment to consider what sensory information and thoughts support your Big Dream. When you have them, focus your senses and your mind on them whenever you think about your Big Dream. Now write this down here or in your notebook.

Sensory support for my Big Dream:

Thought support for my Big Dream:

CHAPTER 5
THE ART OF NON-NEGOTIATION

"They're not fond of rules."

—Rob Siltanen, copywriter, "The Crazy Ones"
ad for Apple computer

"Your time is limited. Don't waste it living someone else's life. Don't be trapped by dogma, which is living the result of other people's thinking. Don't let the noise of other opinions drown your own inner voice. And most important, have the courage to follow your heart and intuition. They somehow already know what you truly want to become. Everything else is secondary."

—Steve Jobs

We all have to negotiate. We all have to compromise. Right? Well, when you're creating your own Reality Distortion Field, the answer is no, you don't.

You see, if you are willing to compromise, this immediately destroys the Reality Distortion Field because the compromise places your idea on a continuum that stretches from the incredibly awesome to the unbelievably bad with the simply mediocre in the middle.

Now, this doesn't mean that you never compromise with anyone, anywhere, anytime. That would be ridiculous. (Although Steve Jobs came very close to achieving the ridiculous in this context.) But when you're pursuing your Big Dream, you can't afford to compromise.

It is your total belief in your Big Dream that creates inspiration in others. This has always been the way with those dreamers who create a Reality Distortion Field. As I said in the first chapter, sometimes these individuals turn out to be crooks selling snake oil. But sometimes they turn out to be the stuff of genius, people like Steve Jobs.

Exercise 6: Creating Certainty

In the quotation at the start of this chapter, Steve Jobs actually explains how you can create the sort of certainty in your mind that will allow you to pursue your dream without compromise, when he says, *"Don't let the noise of other opinions drown out your own inner voice. ... follow your heart."*

To get a sense for how this works, consider something that you absolutely know to be true. You have absolutely no doubt about it. As you think about it, tell yourself that it's true. Notice where that voice of certainty comes from and what it sounds like. Also notice what you feel in your body that lets you know that it's true, that you are totally certain about it. Where do you feel it? How big is the feeling? What size and shape is the feeling? Does the feeling have a color?

Now imagine that someone told you it's not true even though you know it is. As you hear this other person telling you it's not true, do you have any doubts about it? Of course you don't. (By the way, if you are starting to have doubts, then you picked something you were not 100 percent certain about in the first place!)

Notice that as you hear your own inner voice of certainty telling you that it's true, and feeling that feeling that lets you know with complete certainty that it's true, the other voices that cast doubt on that have no impact on you. Notice where these other voices come from and what they sound like.

Now think about your Big Dream. Tell yourself that you will achieve this dream with the same voice of certainty, coming from the same place, as before. Notice as you do so that you get that same feeling within your body letting you know with certainty that you will achieve this goal.

Now imagine someone is casting doubt on your dream or trying to persuade you to compromise. Hear those voices coming from the same place as the doubting voices in the previous exercise. You will notice that they have no effect on you. Record your observations here or in your notebook.

My voice of certainty sounds like this:

My voice of certainty comes from this location:

My voice of certainty has these qualities:

I feel certainty in my body.

Location:

Size:

Shape:

Color:

Doubting voices I know are false sound like this:

Location:

Qualities:

CHAPTER 6
DEALING WITH FAILURE

"Don't lose faith."

—Steve Jobs

"Sometimes when you innovate, you make mistakes. It is best to admit them quickly, and get on with improving your other innovations."

—Steve Jobs

What's the definition of *perfection*? If you think it's doing things perfectly, you're wrong! There is no such thing as perfection in this sense because we all make mistakes. Instead, you can think of perfection as a destination that you can never reach but you can approach. Approaching perfection as closely as humanly possible is the art of paying attention to the mistakes that you make and learning from them, changing how you do things to avoid repeating that mistake in the future.

In fact, this is such an important principle that those who are experts in their field deliberately make mistakes so they can improve. Yes, you heard that right. The best athletes, the best musicians, the best artists, and the best businessmen and women deliberately make mistakes.

10,000 Hour Rule

You may have heard of the 10,000-hour rule formulated by Malcolm Gladwell in his book *Outliers*. This says that to master something, you have to practice for at least 10,000 hours. But what the

10,000-hour rule doesn't say is that if you do practice for 10,000 hours, you will automatically be great.

You may be wondering if you have to practice for 10,000 hours to achieve your Big Dream. Fortunately, the answer is no (and yes). As it turns out, the 10,000-hour rule does not apply equally to all fields. The more structured the field, the more the 10,000-hour rule applies. For example: It would be more applicable to learning classical piano than to playing in a punk-rock band.

So, if your Big Dream is a new idea in a new field that you are defining, you have a lot of scope to set your rules. Having said this, you should treat every experience you have around your Big Dream as learning and practice, including reading this book and completing the exercises.

But it has to be the right kind of practice!

Deliberate Practice

To improve, to master your art, you have to practice just beyond the edge of your ability. If you stay within your current comfort zone, you won't improve very fast, or you may not improve at all. At the same time, it's no use trying to do something that's way beyond you. You'll just end up doing it badly and learning bad habits. To become great, you have to engage in something called *deliberate practice*. Deliberate practice has a number of components, one of the most important is practicing the skill at a level that is possible yet challenging so that mistakes are inevitably made. These mistakes lead to learning, and the learning allows the skill to be practiced at higher and higher levels until mastery is achieved.

To take a simple example: Suppose you want to complete a marathon but you are out of shape and can comfortably run only a mile. If you only ever run a mile, you will never be able to complete the marathon even if you practice for a year. But if you go out and try to run 26 miles straightaway, you will probably injure yourself and will certainly become frustrated. Instead, you should aim to run perhaps a mile and a half. Even if you don't quite manage it, you will have pushed yourself beyond you comfort zone, but not so far that you become injured or frustrated. You can then increase you run to two miles, then three, then five, and so on over time.

It is only through failure that you can reach mastery and approach perfection.

> "I'm convinced that about half of what separates the successful entrepreneurs from the nonsuccessful ones is pure perseverance."
> —Steve Jobs

When you understand that perfection is the art of making mistakes, and noticing what went wrong, then you will begin to welcome the mistakes you make. And when you do, persevering will become as natural to you as breathing.

Now, of course, there will come a day when you fail spectacularly. Something will go terribly wrong. Your business may crash. You may get fired. Steve Jobs himself was fired from Apple following his clash with the board of directors of the company.

> "Sometimes life is going to hit you in the head with a brick. Don't lose faith."
>
> —Steve Jobs

Steve Jobs didn't lose faith when he was fired from Apple. He didn't lose his belief in himself and in the infinite generosity of the universe. Instead, he took some of the money he had made at Apple and invested it in a struggling software company, Pixar.

Now, Steve Jobs's plan when he took over Pixar was to develop a piece of consumer software. He figured if he could design software that people could use to create their own animations, people would find all sorts of amazing ways to use it. Once again he trusted in himself to create an amazing product, and he trusted in the universe to create demand for the product.

As it turned out, he failed—and he failed spectacularly. Nobody wanted his software. But he didn't lose faith, and he persevered. Instead of selling the software as a product, Pixar began to use it to make its own animations. One of the earliest films it made was *Toy Story*. *Toy Story* became a massive success for Pixar. Other films followed. Eventually, Pixar was acquired by Disney. As a result, Steve Jobs became one of the largest shareholders in Disney, making his second fortune in the process.

Pixar would not have been the success it was had Steve Jobs not failed spectacularly at Apple by being fired, and had failed spectacularly in his initial idea for Pixar as a consumer software company.

To succeed with your own Big Dream using your RDF, aim to fail early and often. Go out and deliver your RDF pitch to someone. It doesn't matter who you pitch to. It could be a friend who will give you honest feedback, a total stranger, pretty much anyone. Now, it's important that you don't pitch your RDF to the prospect you really want to impress before you have failed a number of times with others you don' care so much about!

Exercise 7: Failure and Deliberate Practice

After each pitch of your RDF, evaluate your own performance. If you have a friend or colleague who can help with this, or if you can get feedback from your audience, so much the better, as it is notoriously difficult to judge your own performance. In either case, the following questions may be useful to ask yourself. Record the answers here or in your notebook.

• In what area did the audience appear to be *most* engaged?

• In what area did the audience appear to be *least* engaged?

• What is one question someone from the audience asked?

- What was my highest energy level, on a scale of 1 to 10, when it occurred?

- What was my lowest energy level, on a scale of 1 to 10, when it occurred?

- What was the biggest mistake I made?

- What was my the response/feedback from the audience?

   Now consider:

- What was I doing when the audience was most engaged?

- What was I doing when the audience was least engaged?

- How could I have included the answer to the question within my presentation so that I preframed it? (See chapter 8 for preframing.)

- I believe my highest energy was too low/just right/too high.

- I believe my lowest energy was too low/just right/too high.

- Next time I will not make that mistake I will instead do …

- Lesson from audience response/feedback.

Repeat this exercise for each RDF presentation you pitch. Do as many as possible, and make as many mistakes as possible to improve!

CHAPTER 7
THE ART OF OUT FRAMING

"I have a dream."

"I have a dream that one day this nation will rise up and live out the true meaning of its creed: 'We hold these truths to be self-evident: that all men are created equal.'"

—Martin Luther King, Jr.

In the previous section, I described the personal characteristics in your own character. In this section of the book, we will be getting down to specifics, and I will be showing you how to actually construct your own RDF presentation.

In an earlier chapter, we talked about the benefits of aiming for a Big Dream. However, to actually create a Reality Distortion Field for others, it is not enough to simply set a big dream. The first step of actually creating the Reality Distortion Field is to frame the Big Dream in such a way that it becomes irresistible. Steve Jobs did this by using a technique from NLP called *out framing*.

What's important to understand at this stage is that people are never seeking to do what they do. Instead, they're seeking to influence or transform the world around them as a result of what they do.

For example: No one is looking for the cure for cancer. What they are trying to do is to bring health to the lives and families. They may not think about in these terms, and some of them may get lost in their test tubes and equipment, but in all cases, this is why they went into the field.

When you can find the right dream that your idea leads to, then many people will join you without considering whether what you are proposing is possible. And they will join you because they'll buy in to the dream first.

If Martin Luther King, Jr., had simply argued that African Americans should not to face the consequences of the Jim Crow laws, no doubt many people would have agreed with him, but they may not have been inspired in the way they were. And many may have disagreed. Instead, Rev. King challenged the nation to live up to the high ideals of its own Constitution, that all men are created equal. This was a high ideal that everyone could buy in to even if they disagreed with the details of Rev. King's plans.

Steve Jobs used a similar tactic to create his Reality Distortion Field. He didn't preach to his team about building a computer with this much RAM or that much hard drive. Instead, he talked about building "insanely great products."

And when the splits within Apple began that ultimately led to Steve Jobs's departure from Apple, he framed the whole thing as being the pirates against the navy. And, of course, his team of nonconformist computer programmers became the pirates!

Exercise 8: Naming Your Big Dream

So when you're developing your Reality Distortion Field, consider this question: What is the biggest, baddest, most amazing change that could take place in the world as a result of what you're doing? This becomes the title for your Big Dream and your RDF.

Now, when you're talking to people about what you're doing, your goal, use the answer to this question as your first description. You get them to buy in to this, to want it, to want to be a part of it. Because when they buy in, everything else is just details. Record this in your notebook or here.

Title to my Big Dream:

Feel free to play with this title. Come up with five variations:

1. *Title to my Big Dream:*

2. *Title to my Big Dream:*

3. *Title to my Big Dream:*

4. *Title to my Big Dream:*

5. *Title to my Big Dream:*

Which one sounds most compelling? Try the best two or three out on other people. Notice which one lights them up most. You are looking for one that makes them ask you for more information.

When you have one that is totally compelling, try playing with details, changing one or two words. Come up with three variations that are almost the same but subtly different.

1. *Title to my Big Dream:*

2. *Title to my Big Dream:*

3. *Title to my Big Dream:*

Again try each one out and see which one works best with the most people. Once you have it, write it down.

The title to my Big Dream is:

CHAPTER 8
PREFRAMES AND INOCULATION

"The ones who see things differently"

—Rob Siltanen, copywriter, "The Crazy Ones"
ad for Apple computer

Before you deliver your message using your Reality Distortion Field to your chosen audience, test it out first. One reason for doing this is to get some practice, some rehearsal, for the real thing. Another is to have the opportunity to make mistakes and learn from them.

One mistake that you should be particularly interested in is the mistake of not addressing some uncertainty or doubts your audience may have. You will appreciate this type of mistake by listening carefully to the questions your audience asks and the objections they raise.

Now, I know what you've been thinking. You've been wondering how you can deal with the objections that individuals in your audience may have to your message. When somebody raises a valid argument against your idea, you're going to have to start to argue with them, and the rest of the audience will sit back waiting to see who wins.

The Benefits of Preframing

Well, actually, there's a much easier way of doing it that relies on something called *preframing*. When you've mastered the art of preframing, you need never have to deal with this sort of argument again. And knowing that you will never have to deal with this sort of argument, you will never again need to be concerned about how you'll deal with your audience.

The idea behind preframing is very simple: you discover the types of arguments that individuals in your audience may raise, and before you start your delivery, you inoculate the audience against them. You do this by not only explaining why the argument is incorrect but also why it's wrong to even raise the argument in the first place.

Now, does this mean that no one in the audience will be thinking about that argument? Not necessarily. Some people might not be convinced by your preframe. Does it mean that no one in the audience will raise the argument? Well, they're certainly less likely to; but, of course, they still could. What preframing does for you is to prevent the rest of the audience from being affected by the argument one person may raise.

So, you have properly preframed the objection. You can simply refer back to your earlier comments. In fact, if you construct your preframes elegantly, the objection itself will prove to your audience that you are correct!

So, let's show you how to construct your preframes.

Constructing Preframes

As mentioned earlier, first you need to know what arguments are likely to be raised against your big idea: it's too expensive, they don't have time, there's no market for it, the timing isn't right, next year would be better. Whatever these arguments may be, you need to know them upfront. This is why you will discuss your idea with as many people as possible so they can raise any and all possible arguments and objections.

Take all these arguments and objections and distill them down to a few key objection categories. Then for each of these key objections, construct a preframe that goes something like this: *Some people will say [X], and that just means [Y] because [Z].*

Where X is the objection someone might rise against you; Y is the fact that X actually supports your idea; and Z is a reason that links X to Y.

At this point, you're probably saying there can't possibly be a logical and rational reason [Z] that an argument against your idea [X] actually supports your idea [Y].

But it's important to realize that the human brain, for the most part, doesn't think things through logically and rationally. When you understand the scientific concepts underlying preframes, you'll realize that any reason [Z] can be used to support any idea [X] and to undermine any other idea [Y].

One area that psychological researchers are most interested in is *influence*. They're interested in the art of influence because they like to get their research funded by companies that want to influence you to buy things.

One study of influence was carried out inside of a public building where there was a photocopier. Researchers waited until there was a line of people waiting to use the copier. They then sent a researcher to cut into the front of the line.

First, the researchers simply went to the head of the line and said, "Do you mind if I go first?" Around about half the people who were standing in line would let the researchers go first and half wouldn't.

In the second part of the experiment, the researchers went to the head of the line and gave a reason for why they wanted to cut in. They said something like, "Do you mind if I go first because I've got a train to catch and I'm in a rush." This time, more than 90 percent of the people let the researchers go first. After all, they were in a rush; they had a train to catch. It's only polite to let someone go first in that situation, right?

The researchers wanted to discover how important the actual reason was to the result. So they went to the front of the line and said, "Do you mind if I go first because I have to make copies." If you think about this rationally, it is much closer to the first case when they didn't give a reason than to the second case where they gave a good reason. After all, what would you use a photocopier for other than to make copies?

But the amazing result was that virtually the same number of people let them cut in line with the bogus "because I need to make copies" excuse as they did with the valid-sounding, "I have a train to catch." The reason and its connection to the request to cut in made virtually no difference to its effectiveness.

Now, you're probably disagreeing; you're probably thinking that you're not like that, and you wouldn't have let them cut in line. Maybe you're right and you are more rational than the average person. That just means you see the value in this research and can to use it to construct effective preframes.

Examples of Preframing

At this stage, you would probably like to see some examples, so here we go.

Perhaps you believe you don't have anything worth convincing people about; your life goals are limited to being able to pay your rent each month. Using Steve Jobs's RDF principles you can use these seemingly everyday goals to reveal your hidden dreams, the reason you are alive, and by doing so attain your deepest happiness.

Or perhaps you have a dream that is so enormous, so amazing, that you know it's just impossible for you to attain it. If this sounds like you, the RDF is the perfect system to show you how any dream, no matter how large, can be not only possible but totally achievable.

You may be thinking to yourself, "I'm just not influential." If you are, that's exactly why you, more than anyone, will benefit from understanding the secrets of Steve Jobs Reality Distortion Field. Steve Jobs was not born with the ability to transform and create new realities in the minds of others. He learned it. And by applying it, he built up billion-dollar fortunes, not just once, but three times in his relatively short life.

You will recognize these and other preframes from the introduction to this book.

CHAPTER 9
LEVERAGING VALUES

"Do you want a chance to change the world?"

> "Do you want to spend the rest of your life selling sugared water, or do you want a chance to change the world?"

> —Steve Jobs, persuading John Scully to leave Pepsi and join Apple

It's probably safe to say that you want to be persuasive; if you didn't, you wouldn't be reading this book. The question is, *Why* do you want to be persuasive? What will it do for you? Perhaps you're hoping to increase your income and using the money to live your dreams or provide for your future. Perhaps you want the respect that comes from leaving your mark on the world. Or perhaps you want to build better relationships with friends and family, those people who are really significant to you.

Whatever your reason for wanting to be more influential, when you understand how to leverage the power of values, you will automatically become more influential as a result.

John Scully Changes the World

Steve Jobs was a master of crafting his argument to convince the individual in front of him. Perhaps the best example is his recruitment of John Scully to Apple. Scully was working for Pepsi and was considered a master of consumer advertising. But what was he selling? Sugar water. What was his gift to the world? Obesity and cavities? When someone is as talented as John Scully, they like to think they're making a difference, that they're doing something important. It's really hard to hold on to this belief if all you're doing is selling sugar water.

Steve Jobs understood this, either intuitively (because he himself believed he was making a difference to the world) or because he had spent time thinking about it and asking himself what would motivate Scully. Either way, he used this value to change Scully's mind. Scully had been naturally reticent to leave the well-established PepsiCo to join the young and unproven Apple, until Steve Jobs asked him a crucial question: "Do you want to spend the rest of your life selling sugared water, or do you want a chance to change the world?" Scully decided to take the opportunity to change the world and joined Apple.

The Power of Values

When you're able to identify the values of your target audience, you can construct powerful arguments to embed within your Reality Distortion Field.

The power of values arises because values act as powerful heuristics in our decision-making. A *heuristic* is simply a thinking shortcut that evolution has designed to make your life, and the lives of your audience, easier. One example of a heuristic is a brand such as BMW. If you're choosing a car, perhaps engineering, style, and a certain exclusivity are important; consequently, you might choose a BMW. On the other hand, if you are looking for value for money you might buy a Toyota. Or if you consider yourself a patriotic American, you might prefer to buy a Ford, say. Each brand stands for something and makes for easier consumer decision-making. Realizing this, major car companies typically have several brands within their stable, each one appealing to a different group of consumers.

Your values act in much the same way. For example: If you value freedom and you need to decide between several options, the only thing you need to ask myself is which option makes you the most free. You don't need to weigh up all the pros and cons of each option. You just need to consider your overall sense of freedom.

When you use values in this way, you typically do it unconsciously. You don't make a list of how much freer you will be under each of the alternatives; you simply consider each alternative in turn and notice how free you feel. The value freedom is all about the feelings associated with the word *freedom*.

When you can incorporate the values of your audience into your Reality Distortion Field, you will lead them to make decisions emotionally. And when you can take the positive emotions that your audience will feel when considering their own values, and attach these good feelings to your big idea, it will sell itself. Just as Steve Jobs sold Scully on the job at Apple Computers by linking it to Scully's value of changing the world.

Leveraging Values in Practice

The process is pretty simple: the first step is to know your audience's values. If you speak to one person, this is pretty easy. You just engage that person in conversation and find out what he talks about. People will talk about the things that are important to them.

If you're speaking to a group, things can be a little bit more complex, depending upon how diverse the group is. If the group shares common interests or attributes, things are a little easier. All you have to do is to find two or three members of the group who are pretty representative, and have a conversation with them. If they are all from the same corporation or social group, you can also read their website. (Although be warned: a website may not truly reflect the values of the organization, depending upon who wrote it.) In any case, you are listening or looking for their shared values; the values that they all share will most likely be shared by most of the rest of the group as well.

If you're speaking to a large and diverse audience, they will all have different values. What you can do in this case is to make some broad observations about the group and then use very general values that are likely to appeal to them. For example: If you are speaking to a group in a suburban setting, you might want to talk about family values, hard work, caring for children, the importance of friends and neighbors, and so on. If you're speaking to a group in a major metropolitan city, you might want to talk about culture, the arts, social and ethnic diversity, and so on. If you make your values sufficiently general, most people will identify with them.

Even if you don't know your audience at all, you can you can still use universal values, such as freedom, generosity, love, beauty, and so on.

Linking the Values to your Big Dream

Once you know your audience's values, you can begin to link these values to your big idea. There are two main ways of doing this.

1. Your dream = more of their value: The first and most direct way is by explaining how they will have more of that value if they follow your Big Dream.

Supposing you're speaking to an audience from the mountains about the benefits of life insurance. (I'm using this as an example. I'm not suggesting selling life insurance is anyone's Big Dream.) You spent the morning in the town, having breakfast in the diner and speaking to the townsfolk. You come to the conclusion that they value freedom, independence, and self-reliance above everything else.

In constructing your Reality Distortion Field, you must link these values to your message. If they believe that they will have more freedom, independence, and self-reliance as a result of obtaining life insurance, then they will be lining up to sign on the dotted line. For example: Life insurance will provide self-reliance for them and their family should, God forbid, anything happen to them. A maturing life insurance policy will give them independence to enjoy their old age and more financial freedom for their children.

2. Directly linking their value to your idea: The second (and sneakier) way of linking their values to your idea is by remembering that *value* is simply a word that makes us feel good, such as *freedom, independence, self-reliance,* or whatever the relevant values of your audience are. Because the word or words trigger the good feeling, you can attach that feeling to your Big Dream simply by using the word in the sentence.

So you might say: "We are an independent company, and we rely on our own expertize to find the very best policies. You have the freedom to choose the life insurance product that is best suited to you."

You're not suggesting that buying the product will provide them with more freedom; instead, you're suggesting that they have the freedom to buy the product!

Conclusion

Discovering the true values of your audience, and linking these to your big idea, makes delivering your Reality Distortion Field smooth and easy.

Chapter 10
Layering Realities

"One more thing ..."

"Oh, one more thing ..."

—Detective Columbo

"Wait a minute, though; there is one more thing ... "

—Steve Jobs

If you're a student of NLP or Ericksonian hypnosis, you may be familiar with the concept of *open loops* in storytelling. An open loop is a story or metaphor that the storyteller starts but does not finish.

The power of open loops arises from the fact that there is a specific part of your brain responsible for completing tasks. That's why, if you hear a popular ditty, such as "Happy birthday to you/ Happy birthday to you/ Happy birthday dear Mary/ Happy birthday to ..." your brain wants to finish it. In fact, you may have found that your brain added *you* to finish the song!

In contrast, when something is complete, your brain releases a feel-good chemical called *dopamine* that lets you know you have finished. Your brain "relaxes," and its electrical activity goes down. It becomes more open and receptive so that you can begin whatever the next thing you have to do.

That's why the famous TV detective Colombo would always ask his suspect a simple question, appear satisfied with the answer, and turn away—but then turn back and use the line, "Oh, one more thing … ." When the suspect had answered the first question and Columbo turned away, the suspect's brain released a flood of dopamine ("Phew, that was easy!"). His dopamine left the suspect open to Colombo's follow-up question.

Similarly, Steve Jobs would give a presentation showing some amazing new feature of the new product and finish the presentation. But then he would say, "Wait a minute, though; there is one more thing… ." And he would describe an even more amazing feature than the one he had just described. When the audience thought he had finished, their brains released dopamine, leaving them in a highly receptive state for Jobs's follow-up "one more thing" addition.

This simple trick of layering a second benefit or a second question or a second argument on top of the first, just when your audience believes that you have finished, is a very powerful yet simple technique of persuasion.

Oh, and one more thing …

CHAPTER 11
STEALING GROUND

"Great artists steal."

"Picasso had a saying: 'Good artists copy; great artists steal.' And we have always been shameless about stealing great ideas."

—Steve Jobs, stealing a quote from Picasso

One of the more irritating habits that Steve Jobs had, according to his coworkers, was his tendency to appropriate ideas and present them as if they were his own. When a coworker would present him with an idea, he would dismiss it as being completely worthless. But then a few days or a week or so later, he would tell her about it and claimed that it was his own.

This idea of stealing ground was a necessary part of Steve Jobs's lack of compromise. After all, if the idea you steal was yours all along, then you haven't compromised by adopting it!

Of course, there is a significant ethical issue with this principle of "stealing ground." Personally, when I adapt someone else's ideas for my own purposes, I prefer to give that person credit for the original idea. This tends to maintain healthier personal and professional relationships, something that Steve Jobs was not always very good at!

There are also legal considerations when you appropriate somebody else's idea, and indeed Apple has been the target of a number of lawsuits concerning stolen intellectual property. When you appropriate somebody else's idea, you need to make sure you are not in breach of any copyright or similar intellectual property protection laws. Seek qualified legal advice!

Having said this, I know of plenty of people who have become extremely successful in the hypnosis field by appropriating other people's ideas while giving credit where credit is due. At the end of the day, nothing is really new. We stand on the shoulders of the giants who have gone before us.

The real principle is that when you hear about an idea that will add to what you're doing, don't be concerned just because you didn't invent it yourself. Within the appropriate ethical and legal constraints, incorporate it into what you are doing. Steal it and make it your own.

Exercise 9: Stealing Ground, Part 1

Consider your Big Dream:

My Big Dream:

Title of my Big Dream:

Think about people who have achieved greatness in the past, whether in business, sports, the arts, politics, or whatever. List three people here or in your notebook that you particularly admire (these people will become your teachers):

My hero 1:

My hero 2:

My hero 3:

Choose one of these people, and do some research on how he achieved his Big Dream. What actions did he take? Choose five that spanned his career from inception to success and write that down here or in your notebook.

My hero's action 1:

My hero's action 2:

My hero's action 3:

My hero's action 4:

My hero's action 5:

Imagine taking each of these actions yourself. Just allow yourself to daydream and fantasize for now about each. What do you notice about each daydream? Write down your observations here or in your notebook.

Observations about daydream (action 1):

Observations about daydream (action 2):

Observations about daydream (action 3):

Observations about daydream (action 4):

Observations about daydream (action 5):

Now imagine you are watching a movie in which your hero adopts your Big Dream. How does he begin to implement it? Write your observations here or in your notebook.

Observations about my hero activating my Big Dream:

You may want to repeat this exercise with some of the other heroes you noted above. Notice what you learn from each using the outline above. What common threads do you begin to notice? What can you steal from these teachers?

Exercise 9: Stealing Ground, Part 2

Give your RDF pitch to someone. Ask her what she thinks. Steal any good ideas she raises!

CHAPTER 12
PHYSIOLOGY OF RDF

"My father taught me things about body language that psychologists have been catching up with ever since. He always knew when I was lying because my posture was all wrong"

—Richard Griffiths

Now that you have constructed your Reality Distortion Field, you have to deliver it to your audience. In this section of the book, I will offer five keys to presenting your RDF in a way that will have most impact.

Physiology Big and Small

Your audience may be an audience of one or an audience of thousands. The bigger the audience you are speaking to, the more flamboyant you can afford to be with your gestures. The smaller and more intimate your audience, the more you may want to dial back the flamboyance of your gestures. If you are speaking for the benefit of the camera, you may wish to imagine your delivery is one on one with each member of your potential audience.

Research suggests that most of a spoken message is delivered unconsciously. This means it's delivered with your body language and your voice, not just with your words.

The most famous research was that done by Dr. Albert Mehrabian, who studied the idea of *congruency* in face-to-face communication. Congruency is when *what* you say and *how* you say it send the same message. Dr. Mehrabian found that when what was said was not supported by how it was said, the listeners would pay much more attention to body language and the tone of voice than what a person is actually saying—a lot more attention. Dr. Mehrabian found that when it came to congruency, a massive 55 percent of communication is contained in body language, 38 percent in tone of voice, and only 7 percent in the actual words used.

So, making sure that your physiology and body language and your tone of voice support your message is absolutely key to building a strong Reality Distortion Field!

Now I am going to give you some ideas about the kinds of physiology and voice tone you can use to support your Reality Distortion Field.

However, because most of your nonverbal communication (body language and voice tone) is unconscious, it's simply impossible to control everything you do consciously. What you're going to find is that when you're busy delivering your message, it's impossible to pay attention to all the details of your body language and tone of voice at the same time. So, I'm going to give you a much easier way of going about it, based on your emotional state in the next chapter.

But before I do that, I will give you a few ideas for specific types of physiology you might want to use in delivering your Reality Distortion Field. These are based upon the Satir categories of NLP.

The Leveler

The Leveler has a balanced and level physiology. Whether standing or sitting, his feet will be shoulder width and parallel, with his weight firmly rooted to the earth. He will have an upright posture and raised head. Great statesmen and orators, such as John F. Kennedy or Winston Churchill, used the Leveler when giving their speeches.

Gestures are symmetrical. The palms of your hands will be either facing down, as if you're placing your ideas solidly on the ground, or facing toward each other, as if you're holding your ideas between your hands.

Your gaze will be level and steady, holding the eyes of each member of your audience for a moment or two before moving on to the next.

In the Leveler, your voice will be midtone, authoritative, and certain.

In summary, the Leveler is a great physiology for projecting authority and certainty.

The Distractor

The Distractor is everything that the Leveler is not. The Distractor, physiology, is used by great communicators who can thoroughly engage with their audience. Examples include energetic comedians, such as Robin Williams, and truly inspirational speakers, such as Tony Robbins.

The Distractor has an asymmetrical physiology. Weight is shifted onto one foot or the other. The body and head move around, first to one side then to the other, or first forward and then backward.

Gestures too will be asymmetrical, perhaps raising just the right arm or just the left. The hands may open or close, the fingers spreading to throw out energy, or the fists closing to capture it.

Your face will be animated, your eyes open in surprise or focusing with concentration.

In the Distractor, your voice will be excited an animated as you share your enthusiasm with the audience.

In summary, the Distractor is a great physiology for sharing passion and excitement with your audience.

The Visionary

The Visionary is inspirational because she sees things that other people cannot. You can find examples in great preachers and spiritual saints. Think of Martin Luther King, Jr., as one example.

The Visionary is in some ways similar to the Leveler: the Visionary is centered inside herself and projects a sense of certainty. But rather than engaging directly with the audience, the Visionary describes that vision, her Big Dream.

As a result of the Visionary's ability to see things that are hidden from everybody else, she tends to look up toward the heavens, toward the vision that only she can see. Her gestures also reach up toward this vision, at least long enough to grasp it so she can offer it to her audience.

The tone of his voice is richer and carries more energy than the Leveler's does, but without the quickness of the Distractor.

In summary, the Visionary is a great physiology for sharing your vision when that vision is important and beneficial for the world.

You may wish to become expert in one of these styles of delivery, or you may want to move between them, perhaps using the Distractor to engage your audience, the Visionary to introduce them to your Big Dream, and the Leveler to describe how you intend to realize that Big Dream.

CHAPTER 13
THE SECRET OF CONGRUENCE

" To be yourself in a world that is constantly trying to make you something else is the greatest accomplishment. "

—Ralph Waldo Emerson

The key to truly mastering your physiology in delivering your RDF is to realize that your body language and physiology and the tone of your voice arise out of your *emotional* state. They're not really consciously controlled at all. When you step into the right emotional state, your body language and tone of voice will reflect that state.

Exercise 10: The Circle of Excellence

To step into your ideal emotional state, we will use an exercise from NLP called *the circle of excellence*. The circle of excellence exercise uses active imagination to begin to stimulate your unconscious mind to generate your ideal state.

It's very simple: All you have to do is to imagine a circle on the ground in front of you. Do that now: imagine a circle on the ground in front of you. Notice what color the circle is, if you see a color. The circle needs to be big enough for you to step into, large enough to be comfortable to stand inside, and close enough that you can step into it easily.

Now imagine all the emotional resources you will need to deliver your message. You get to decide what these emotional resources are, but I am going to give you a few ideas to start.

Firstly, you'll want a feeling of certainty that your idea is totally awesome. I showed you some ways of building this belief earlier in the book, so you can incorporate these into your circle of excellence. Take a look at your circle, and imagine you see your future self in the circle looking absolutely certain that your idea is totally awesome. Notice what this future self looks like, how this future self is standing, how this future self is breathing that reflects the sense of certainty. Make the picture brighter and a little bigger so you can easily step inside it. When it's just perfect, go ahead and step inside the circle, inside that future you, and feel how good that feels. When you're ready, you can step outside of the circle again. Take a look at the circle, and notice what color it is now.

You're going to want to have some confidence in yourself, confidence in your ability to implement this idea, and confidence in your ability to persuade your audience. Take a look at the circle again, and notice your future self standing there. You see your future self standing there with that sense of certainty in the awesomeness of your Big Dream, but this time also with absolute self-confidence, self-confidence in your ability to make your dream a reality and to persuade your audience. Notice how your future self is standing and breathing. Make the picture brighter and a little bigger, and when you're ready, step inside it. Notice how good it feels. When you're ready step out of the circle, take a look at the circle again noticing how the circle has changed. Perhaps it's a different color, or maybe it's simply brighter.

Continue to add more resources into the circle. You might want to consider such resources as:

- Sense of humor

- Unlimited energy

- Patience

- Flexibility

Whatever resources you feel would help you in communicating with your audience, place them one by one into the circle. See your future self with that resource, make the picture bigger and brighter, and then step into it and feel how good it feels. Each time you step out of the circle look back and notice how the color of the circle has changed.

When you have placed every resource you want into the circle, you can also pick it up and put it into your pocket and take it with you wherever you go!

Exercise 11: Amping Things Up

A problem that everyone encounters when making presentations to an audience is that our emotional state almost always feels bigger from the inside than it looks from the outside.

If you don't believe me, I invite you to video yourself making a short presentation, maybe something as simple as telling an entertaining story from your life at an appropriate level of animation.

Now record yourself telling the same story, but this time throw in twice the energy you did the first time.

Finally, tell the same story for a third time, this time pulling out all the emotional stops and going totally over the top.

Next, watch each version of your story. (If you have never seen yourself on video, this can be disturbing!) Most people surprise themselves with how listless they look in their usual emotional level and how much more impactful they appear the second and third times they tell the story as their emotional energy increases.

Get used to the emotional feeling that corresponds with your most impactful presentations so that you can step into the most appropriate level of energy for any presentation and any part of your presentation.

CHAPTER 14
PAYING ATTENTION TO YOUR AUDIENCE

"Everything has beauty but not everyone sees it."

--Confucius

There is something magical about a human connection. Even though you can buy virtually anything online, you probably still choose to go into brick-and-mortar stores and speak to real people for many things. We are much more likely to buy something when we are face to face with a real person.

One important aspect of this human connection—in fact, the key aspect—is eye contact. After all, the eyes are not called the windows of the soul for nothing.

It's important to realize that eye contact is an experience that takes place *between* you and another person or *between* you and a group of people if you're speaking to an audience. By making and maintaining eye contact, you *send* energetic information to the other person, and you *receive* energetic information from that person.

When you look into the eyes of the people in the audience, they're more likely to believe you, to believe in you, and to be convinced by you. And you see whether they are being convinced so that you can adjust your Reality Distortion Field accordingly.

Exercise 12: Tapping into Peripheral Vision, Part 1

When you're speaking to a group, it is important that you make eye contact with each individual. It's also important that you see the group as a whole. Fortunately, your eye is uniquely well designed for this task. By using your peripheral vision, you can continuously track the group as a whole. At the same time, you can use your foveal vision to look at, and connect with, each individual in turn.

Here's an easy exercise to build this split-attention skill.

Look at the wall in front of you, and choose some spot on that wall. If you're outside, look into the distance, and choose an object to focus on. Keeping your eyes on that spot and without moving your head, begin to notice the area around it. Then begin to notice the whole of the wall (if you're inside). Then begin to notice the whole of the room or space around you. To do this, you will have to pay conscious attention to your peripheral vision.

Now bring your attention back to that single spot, and once more widen your gaze out to take in the area around it, the whole of the wall, and the whole of the room around you. Practice this until you can easily and naturally tune into your peripheral vision.

Exercise 12: Tapping into Peripheral Vision, Part 2

Do the next part of the exercise when you're in a public place or with a partner. Look at the person or group of people, and expand your awareness into peripheral vision. When you have done so, notice that you can move your attention around within your field of awareness.

What I mean by this is that you can be looking straight ahead while being aware of the whole of the space around you. Then you can shift your *awareness* to the left side then to the right side without moving your eyes from straight ahead.

When you've got the idea of this, you can look at a group of people and expand your awareness out into peripheral vision and then bring your attention back in to "wrap around" the group. It should feel as though you are giving the group an energetic hug. Eventually, you will also be able to remain in peripheral vision while moving your head, your gaze, and your body. It takes little bit of practice, but it's well worthwhile in developing this skill if you are going to be speaking to groups.

CHAPTER 15
KEEPING YOUR OUTCOME IN MIND

"Keep the end in mind."

—Steven Covey,
*The 7 Habits of
Highly
Successful People*

All great communicators and influencers share one important habit. Successful entrepreneurs and businesspeople share the same habit. So do great sportsmen, scientists, artists, and musicians.

That habit is to keep your outcome literally in mind as you go about your business.

You see, a part of your brain acts as the interface between your conscious and unconscious minds. Properly used, it allows your conscious mind to easily and accurately direct the vast resources and power of your unconscious in the direction of your outcome.

This interface is called your *working memory* by neuroscientists. In this chapter, we will describe what working memory is, how to use it, and specifically how to use it to create a Reality Distortion Field.

Working Memory

Working memory consists of three inter-related parts of your brain:

1. Your visual cortex applied to internal images, meaning what you see in your mind's eye

2. Your auditory cortex, used to play remembered or internally generated sounds

3. The meaning-making part of your brain that creates a meaning or title to the "movie"

So you have:

1. A movie screen

2. A soundtrack

3. A movie title

The combination of the above three elements constitutes your working memory.

How to Use Working Memory

To use working memory to achieve your outcomes, you simply choose what you want and find an inspiring way to describe or label this outcome. This will become the movie title. You then picture this outcome in your mind's eye. Make the picture big and bright. Bring it close to you. Make it three-dimensional.

Now add a fantastic soundtrack. This could be dialogue, music, an angelic choir—whatever is appropriate and inspiring to you.

Playing this movie in your mind, in your working memory, as you go about your tasks will instruct your unconscious mind as to what you want to have happen. Your unconscious mind will then bring its virtually unlimited resources to bear to make that a reality.

How *Not* to Use Working Memory

Unfortunately, many of us use working memory backwards. We imagine all the things that could go wrong. We then add a depressing sound track, often a whiney or depressed voice. We finally add a horrible title, "My Life Sucks." This a truly self-destructive way to use your working memory!

Working Memory and the Reality Distortion Field

Working memory plays a key role in creating your Reality Distortion Field and delivering it to your chosen audience. You will already have an image of your chosen nonconsensus reality built from earlier steps in the RDF process. All you have to do now is to add to your movie a picture of your audience nodding in agreement as they listen to your obvious truth.

In this movie, everything the audience does or says supports your truth even if it's not immediately obvious how.

A great example of this is when Steve Jobs was taking questions from Apple employees and got ambushed by a question (www.youtube.com/watch?v=FF-tKLISfPE). The questioner tells Jobs that he has destroyed everything great at Apple. After a few moments fumbling for the appropriate response, Jobs tells the man that he is absolutely right. Jobs then goes on to explain why everything the questioner has said actually supports what he has done at Apple.

If Jobs had been carrying round a picture of the questioner being his enemy, he would have responded with anger, telling the man why he was wrong. You see Jobs almost move in this direction at the start of his answer. But instead, Jobs focuses on the image that the questioner is supporting him. He just has to allow his mind enough time to settle and then to see how the question supports Jobs's position.

Exercise 13: Using Working Memory

Select something that you would like someone to do for you. Start with something that's easy and not too important—perhaps asking for assistance in a store or asking a coworker for help.

Whatever it is, make a picture in your mind of the outcome you want. Maybe it's a short movie of the person saying, "Of course, I'd be delighted to help." Make the picture big and bright. Bring it close; make it three-dimensional, as if you were inside it.

Add a soundtrack to the movie. Something inspirational. Add richness and warmth to the voices of you and the other person.

Choose a great title, one that implies a win-win outcome for you and the other person: "How We Solved the Problem Together," perhaps.

Now, keep that movie, soundtrack, and title in mind and go ask the person for help. No matter what her response is, keep the movie of your outcome big and bright in your mind with the soundtrack and title. If you have to, ask again in a different way. Remember the person with the most flexibility controls the situation.

Practice this a number of times on easy things. When you feel comfortable you have it down, move on to something more important, like asking you boss for a raise.

When this process becomes second nature to you, you can easily incorporate it into your RDF presentations.

CHAPTER 16
PUTTING IT TOGETHER

"All you have to do to bring about this impossible dream for the world is to fully and completely step into it yourself."

—Shawn Carson

In this chapter, you will get the chance to combine everything from earlier chapters into building an incredible Reality Distortion Field of your own.

Exercise 14

Step 1: Aim for the impossible.

Ask yourself what you want to do. Once you have that as your goal, make it bigger, more ambitious.

Now ask yourself, What is the benefit of doing this for other people? This could mean either that you will it do for other people or that if other people were to do it too, what would it do for them? Once you have this, make it bigger again, more beneficial.

Now imagine everyone in the world gets to experience this benefit. How would the world be different? Multiply this benefit to the world by 10.

This is your Big Dream. Now write this down here or in your notebook.

My Big Dream:

Step 2: Build your locus of control.

Remember, all you have to do to bring about this impossible dream for the world is to fully and completely step into it yourself. Then take the next smallest step in that direction, trusting the universe to provide the opportunities you need to succeed. Take the next smallest step, then "wash, rinse, repeat." Write this down here or in your notebook.

My next smallest step is:

Step 3: Do *not* negotiate your Big Dream.

If it's really important to you, then it's not for sale.

My Big Dream is important to me because:

Step 4: Construct your nonconsensus reality.

Focus on experiences and facts that support your Big Dream. This builds your belief. Write this down here or in your notebook.

The experiences that support my Big Dream are:

The facts that support my Big Dream are:

Step 5: Fail early and often.

The only way to achieve your Big Dream is to fail repeatedly. When Thomas Edison was asked how it felt to have failed 1,000 times to make the light bulb, he replied he hadn't failed a thousand times, he hadn't even failed once—he had found a thousand ways how **not** to make a light bulb. Incidentally, one of those "failures" led to the invention of the cathode ray tube, and to the invention of the television!

Step 6: Express your big dream as something that will change the world.

People want to change the world and will buy in to your Big Dream when they understand how it will do so.

How my Big Dream will change the world:

Step 7: Inoculate your audience using preframes.

Identify common objections to your Big Dream. Explain why these objections make your Big Dream inevitable, before your audience even thinks about them. Write this down here or in your notebook.

Common objections to my Big Dream could include:

I will preframe these objections like this:

Step 8: Leverage values.

Identify the values held by your audience, and leverage these by including them in your description of your Big Dream.

My audiences' values may include:

Step 9: "One more thing ..."

Save your best for last.

My one more thing will be:

Steps 10: Deliver your RDF.

Use you entire self to deliver your RDF. Use your physiology, emotional state, your eyes and other senses, and your mind to make your presentation compelling. Fill in the blanks following.

Other role models are:

I am aware of how my emotions and states influence my congruency. The emotional states I choose are:

1.

2

3.

I will use the following Satir categories within my presentation:
Leveler

Distractor

Visionary

I am practiced at using peripheral vision and can see the entire group.

My working memory is positive and supports the outcome of my Big Dream:

The movie is:

The soundtrack is:

The title is:

I will practice delivering my Big Dream to these people:

1.

2.

3.

on this day:

In this place:

90

I will practice delivering my Big Dream to these people:

1.

2.

3.

on this day:

In this place:

I will practice delivering my Big Dream to these people:

1.

2.

3.

on this day:

In this place:

I will deliver my Big Dream to these people:

1.

2.

3.

On this day:

In this place:

CONCLUSION

"It's never to late to be who you might have been."

—George Elliot

This book is written for ordinary people with Big Dreams, dreams about making the world a better place. By mastering the Reality Distortion Field, you can become amazingly persuasive and make an incredible difference to those around you. But it works only as long as you embrace a win-win attitude.

And it works only if you act!

We have offered you many exercises in this book, some simple, some more difficult. Start with the easy ones and build from there. But start. Start today if you haven't already.

You have a unique genius inside you. And the world needs you to make a difference.

Other Books By This Publisher

The Swish
By Shawn Carson and Jess Marion

The Visual Squash
By Jess Marion and Shawn Carson

The BEAT Coaching System
By Sarah and Shawn Carson

The Meta Pattern
By Shawn and Sarah Carson

Deep Trance Identification: Unconscious Modeling and Mastery for Hypnosis Practitioners, Coaches, and Everyday People
By Shawn Carson and Jess Marion with John Overdurf

Deep Trance Identification Companion
By Shawn Carson and Jess Marion with John Overdurf

Quit: The Hypnotist's Handbook to Running Effective Stop Smoking Sessions
By Jess Marion, Sarah Carson, and Shawn Carson

Keeping the Brain in Mind: Practical Neuroscience for Coaches, Therapists, and Hypnosis Practitioners
By Shawn Carson and Melissa Tiers

Tree of Life Coaching: Practical Secrets of the Kabbalah for Hypnosis and NLP Practitioners and Coaches
By Shawn Carson

I Quit: Stop Smoking Easily Through the Power of Hypnosis
By Jess Marion, Sarah Carson, and Shawn Carson

HypnoGames for HypnoJunkies
By Sarah Carson, Jess Marion, and Shawn Carson

From Call To Client
By Jess Marion, Sarah Carson and Shawn Carson

Small Thoughts For Big Change: 21 Beliefs To Create Magic In Your Life
Sarah Carson, Shawn Carson and Jess Marion

Have Mercy: 21 Tales To Transform Your Life
Mercedes Herman

For more information visit us at
www.theintelligenthypnotist.com

www.ingramcontent.com/pod-product-compliance
Lightning Source LLC
Chambersburg PA
CBHW071417040426
42445CB00012BA/1179